2024

YOUth&I

Issue 4

YOUth&I acknowledges the Ngunnawal and Ngambri people, who are the Traditional Custodians of the land on which this book was created.

We pay our respects to Elders past, present and emerging.

We acknowledge that the land is stolen land, which we benefit from occupying, and that sovereignty was never ceded.

YOUth&I extends this acknowledgement to all First Nations peoples around the world on whose lands these entries were created.

Editor-in-chief: **Steph Lum**
Stakeholder manager: **Georgia Andrews**
Design and layout: **Gabrielle Niemeyer**
Front cover: **Olympia Balopitos**
Internal art: **Intersex community members of A Gender Agenda**

Website: https://youthandi.org/
Contact: info@youthandi.org

ISBN: 978-0-6456726-2-6
ISSN: 2653-6641 (online)
ISSN: 2653-6633 (print)

Special thanks to our translators who have helped make it possible to publish works from around the world: Laura Inter, Free, Kon Zer and Leonor Patino Oropeza. We have tried to translate faithfully the original texts though at times have preferenced keeping essence and style over a literal translation.

This anthology includes themes of coerced medical intervention and IGM (intersex genital mutilation), trauma, suicidality and nudity.

YOUth&I gratefully acknowledges the support of Intersex Human Rights Australia for funding this project.

Foreword

Welcome to Issue 4 of YOUth&I, an intersex youth anthology that celebrates the creative works of young intersex people from around the world. YOUth&I is a publication by and for intersex people. In this issue, we are proud to share with you poems, song lyrics, prints, photographs, drawings and essays, including many translated works. YOUth&I actively welcomes pieces in languages other than English to ensure voices not heard as often can still be shared. We work with intersex contributors to translate their works and publish the original and its translation together so as not to lose their words and meaning.

People with intersex variations are often misunderstood. Particularly as young intersex people we are often told who we are, what our desires are and what we will want in the future. These things are assumed about us. Then our bodies are changed for us. Intersex people around the world are still routinely subject to non-consensual medical interventions, hormonal and surgical, to change our bodies to appear more *normal* – with the assumption of what is best for us. When performed without information, consent, and connection with other intersex people, we are forced into bodies to make other people more comfortable and told to act in a way they think we should live. We continue to fight for this to change by sharing our stories of who we are. *My existence on its own is an act of resistance – IR-Is.*

YOUth&I is based on Ngunnawal and Ngambri land, in Canberra, ACT, Australia. Since the last issue of YOUth&I, the Australian Capital Territory (ACT) has passed world-leading legislation to restrict medical interventions on intersex people (people with variations in sex characteristics) without consent. This represents a huge step forward in protecting our bodily autonomy, empowering us to make decisions over our own bodies, and recognising the importance of psychosocial support for us and our families. We hope that this legislation provides a model for other countries around the world, offers a chance for societies to learn, grow and include all people with variations in sex characteristics and other kinds of bodily diversity. *I wanted to ensure that others like me wouldn't have to endure the same struggles alone – Noor Alom.*

This issue's theme, *Grow*, captures this idea of learning and change. Learning about who we are, that other people like us exist, and learning from our experiences and those of intersex people around us to help us grow in new ways. *Could I dare dream the thought, that this isn't me? – Max Aurora.* By learning how to live with our bodies in places that can treat us cruelly, we grow from these experiences and connections with others in new and sometimes unexpected ways. I am not a flower, but I can learn to treat myself like one. *I can be exactly what I am and not have to apologise for the way I grow – Mouse.* In this issue we also reflect on who we want to become and how we can get there. We take back our agency and create our own futures. *Always remember that it's never too late to do things right – Lee.* This issue captures our different relationships with ourselves over time and embraces who we are and our intention for the future.

YOUth&I is also growing. We give our great thanks to Intersex Human Rights Australia (IHRA) who have generously funded this issue of YOUth&I. From an initial ACT government grant in 2019, to ongoing support from IHRA since then, YOUth&I is now an imprint of newly formed Orchid Paper Press, an independent publisher based on Ngunnawal and Ngambri land specialising in intersex stories. By sharing our stories, we make intersex people visible. Thank you to our translators for helping us elevate the voices of intersex people no matter where they live. And of course, thank you most of all to our young intersex people. Thank you for sharing your heart and your courage with the world.

Steph Lum, Editor-in-chief
November 2024

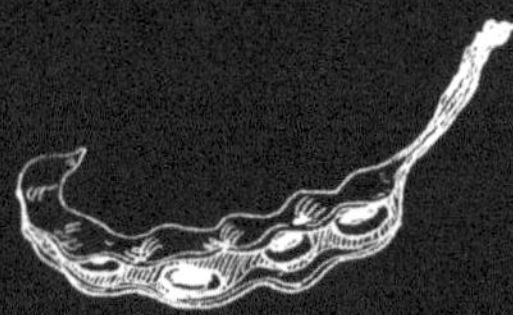

In memory of Shivol Shoko
Intersex activist, member of Intersex Community of Zimbabwe, friend

Meet me at the intersection of what was
And the promise of what will be
The place where moments stretch
With timeless immediacy
Look, look up—it's hope's best side
Hold my hand and jump
Let's turn our backs to before
And tomorrow, we'll be free

Contents

1-3
Foreword

6
The Ballerine, the Poet and the Curtain
M. Hill

7
Ko Ira Tangata Tēnei Taniwha //
This Taniwha is Intersex
Tobias Kenny

8
Untangling
Max Aurora

9
H.U.M.A.N
Juniper Fox

10-12
Crecer: Sin etiquetas
IR-Is

13-15
Growing: Without labels
IR-Is

17
Joy is a new dress I haven't had the courage to put on yet
ITSH

18
Grow through emotions
Ciara

19
Gender is over
Ranzie Orcena

20-22
Me falta un cromosoma, me sobran ganas de vivir
Marel

23-25
I'm missing a chromosome, but I have plenty of desire to live
Marel

26-27
Together we bloom
Kon Zer

28
Fut—Lego mis favoritos //
Soccer—Lego my favourites
Vanessy

29
My intersex flag
Nico

30
Inusual
Free

31
Unusual
Free

32
Crecer juntos //
Growing together
Ayito

33
Existen personas Intersex, que también son trans //
There are intersex people who are also trans
Ayito

34-35
From Shubhra to Noor-Alom: My Journey of Resilience and Empowerment
Noor Aloom

36-37
Crecer
Azucena

38-39
Growing up
Azucena

41
I n b e t w e e n
Juniper Fox

42-45
Surviving
Healing
Censurable
Mel Kurutta

46
Evolución
Yela

47
Evolution
Yela

49
Grow
Lee

51
Baby teeth
ITSH

52-56
AO
Otto Etraud & Kali

57
I find myself in flowers
Mouse

58-59
Excerpts from *Microrretalos sobre Intersexualidad*
Rosalinda & Mary

60
Crecer //
Growing up
A.A

61
Only a dead man should lose hope
Lee

62-63
Soliloquio:
Fragmentos de un Cuerpo Infinito
Julian

64-65
Soliloquy:
Fragments of an Infinite Body
Julian

66-69
About the contributors

The Ballerine, the Poet and the Curtain

M. Hill

The dancers jump, spin, and bend in conjunction

But I am on the side

I cannot jump, spin, nor bend with them

For I am a poet

For I am not allowed on stage

I am hidden behind the curtain

But still, I am an artist

My words can jump, spin, and bend

Just like the dancers

Ko Ira Tangata Tēnei Taniwha

Tobias Kenny

This Taniwha is Intersex

The image is of a taniwha, a mythological Māori creature, which have been both protectors and instigators of mischief. The taniwha has a range of sexual characteristics, some relating to my own characteristics, and others I do not have. The term 'ira tangata' is a contemporary term for Māori who are intersex.

Untangling

Max Aurora

How do you write a song about untangling?
The stages and denial undone
A tidal wave returning with every tide
To sit with the emotion each time

How do you write a song about untangling?
The storm fronts inside of your brain
One of the old gripping to remain
Another a place asking for change

This is my untangling

How do you ask for help when you're alone?
To reach out in the dark and answer the phone?
Over the years, I've been told no
Stay where you are, be what you're told

This is my untangling

When I look in my drawers
Do I like what I see?
Could I dare dream the thought,
That this isn't me?

This is my untangling
This is my...

I stare at the valley
At twilight and dawn
My eyes wide open like a fawn
The patterns unfolding
Help me convalesce

I am intersex and have a variation called 'XX testicular difference of sexual development' or 'XX male' for short. I wrote these lyrics one urgent night when I decided to change from being on Testosterone HRT to Estrogen. Very soon later I turned it into a song (which will be released in late 2024).

H.U.M.A.N

Juniper Fox

Crecer: Sin etiquetas

IR-Is

"Desde que tengo memoria, simplemente existir ha sido un desafío constante."

Mi realidad es un concepto que otras personas entienden a partir de múltiples identidades interrelacionadas: mujer, afrodescendiente, inmigrante, y me he visto obligada a luchar constantemente por el derecho a reclamar mi humanidad y simplemente ser. Cada uno de estos nombres ha sido un yugo pesado que ha limitado mi capacidad de florecer y me ha obligado a intentar demostrar mi inocencia en un mundo que me condenó desde el principio.

Como persona intersexual, mi cuerpo y mi integridad han sido objeto de un examen despiadado. Fui sometida a cirugías "correctivas" que intentaron cambiar mi anatomía para ajustarse al estándar binario de género durante toda mi infancia, lo que dejó cicatrices físicas y emocionales que aún duelen profundamente en mi corazón. Crecer sabiendo que mi cuerpo es visto como un error, algo que necesita ser "arreglado", fue lo que impulsó mi lucha por reclamar mi integridad y mi derecho a existir.

Además, mi existencia como mujer racializada en una sociedad que solo otorga privilegios a lo blanco y lo masculino ha significado cargar con el peso de múltiples estereotipos y conceptos erróneos que intentan despojarme de mi humanidad. He sido exotizada, hipersexualizada y reducida a meros constructos que niegan mi individualidad. Deambular por este mundo bajo la percepción de "la otra", la intrusa, ha exigido una fortaleza inquebrantable para mantener mi dignidad intacta frente a las miradas acusatorias y los comentarios hirientes que siempre caían como una avalancha.

Y, sin embargo, a pesar de los desafíos, tuve que enfrentar mi nueva realidad. Arrancada de mi tierra natal por la violencia y la persecución, y obligada a un viaje lleno de peligros e incertidumbres, siempre fui tratada como una carga, como una marginada que buscaba privilegios que no estaban destinados para ella. La imposibilidad de encontrar un trabajo decente y llevar una vida estable se convirtió en un recordatorio constante de mi vulnerabilidad y de la precariedad que definía todo mi ser, dejándome al margen de una sociedad que se negaba a acogerme.

"Eres negra, no te maquilles, no te arregles, no vistas bien, no hables, no nos muestres lo que has estudiado. Eres intersexual. No puedo ayudarte, no podemos hacer nada por ti, no tienes nada, lo tienes todo, vete, no, aquí no, afuera, no, allí tampoco, come del suelo, haz lo que digo, agacha la cabeza, agáchala, agáchala..."

Me siguen arrebatando mi autonomía y mi derecho a elegir sobre mi propio cuerpo. Mis necesidades y experiencias reales se relegan a favor de una agenda que solo intenta encajarme en categorías binarias.

Y si a eso se le añade ser una mujer negra, la carga se vuelve aún más pesada. Mi color de piel, mi ascendencia caribeña, mis rasgos físicos y mi cuerpo convergen en el foco de un estigma que me etiqueta como "indeseable", que me ve como alguien que no pertenece, que "debería regresar a su país" o que debería contentarse con lo que le suceda. Ni siquiera estando en el "aquí y ahora" puedo escapar de los prejuicios y la discriminación que marcaron mi realidad desde el primer día.

Me encontré relegada a los márgenes, a los espacios más peligrosos y vulnerables. Mi ser intersexual y mi raza se convirtieron en baluartes inquebrantables entre yo y una vida decente, entre yo y mis sueños y aspiraciones. Se me ve como "la otra", la intrusa que tiene que contentarse con las migajas que la sociedad desea arrojarle. Mi dolor físico y emocional, producto de una infancia llena de violencia médica y una adultez marcada por los intentos recurrentes de sobrevivir, se relegan a un segundo plano en favor de una supuesta "igualdad" que no hace más que perpetuar mi condición de ser desechable.

Y, sin embargo, me niego a aceptar este destino. Mi existencia en sí misma es un acto de resistencia, un desafío al sistema que insiste en negarme mi humanidad. Me aferro a mi dignidad y a mis esperanzas, convirtiéndome en una voz que se niega a ser silenciada. Crezco a partir de mi determinación y de mi convicción en el hecho de que merezco vivir en este mundo. Y a través de este crecimiento también encuentro la fuerza para seguir luchando, para seguir trazando un camino que, aunque sinuoso, sé que llevará a un horizonte lleno de igualdad e inclusión.

He aprendido a abrazar la complejidad de mí misma, a encontrar fuerza donde los demás ven debilidad. He descubierto que mi intersexualidad no es una condición, sino una forma legítima de estar viva, una expresión de la diversidad humana que merece ser apreciada. He reclamado mi derecho a ser mujer en mis propios términos, sin someterme a los estándares impuestos por una sociedad que siempre está juzgando y rechazando.

Y he endurecido mi resistencia contra toda forma de estereotipación u objetificación.

"Mi existencia en sí misma es un acto de resistencia"

Mi voz se alza como una declaración jurada de mi capacidad para florecer incluso en las condiciones más difíciles, un grito que se niega a ser acallado o borrado. Crecer en estas circunstancias me forjó como una luchadora implacable, una sobreviviente que se aferra a su propio valor y esperanza, incluso cuando este mundo parece empeñado en negar su derecho a existir.

Sé que mi lucha no es solo mía, sino que también pertenece a aquellos que, como yo, han sido desplazados a los márgenes. A pesar de que mi cuerpo ha sido objeto de tanto escrutinio y manipulación, y a pesar de que mi piel ha sido motivo de estigma y rechazo, mi espíritu permanece intacto. Con una valentía forjada en la adversidad, me paro frente al mundo entero y alzo mi voz para exigir el derecho que tengo sobre quien soy, sin vergüenza ni miedo. Porque la intersexualidad no es una identidad o un género, es una variación biológica natural que merece ser celebrada y respetada.
E incluso en medio de esta batalla, anhelo un futuro donde mi existencia no sea algo que provoque polémica o rechazo, sino algo que se acepte y valore. Sueño con el día en que pueda caminar libremente y sin miedo, sin tener que justificarme o esconder quién soy. Y de esta manera, con cada paso que doy, con cada historia que comparto, mi cuerpo intersexual florece como un acto de obstinada resistencia, desafiando los límites de lo que la sociedad considera "normal". Crecer en un mundo que insiste en mantenernos pequeños es, en sí mismo, un acto subversivo, es tomar las riendas de nuestras propias narrativas y reformular el concepto de humanidad. Me niego a aceptar las etiquetas, los diagnósticos, los intentos de definirme. Soy mucho más que eso. Soy una constelación de posibilidades, una sinfonía de variaciones, un lienzo en constante evolución. Al crecer, amplío mi existencia y me convierto en un faro de esperanza para aquellos que, como yo, se atreven a desafiar las convenciones y exigen su derecho a vivir plenamente como son.

Growing: Without labels

IR-Is

> "Since I can remember, simply existing has been a constant challenge."

My reality is a concept that other people understand from multiple interlinked identities— female, afro-descendant, immigrant— and I've been forced to constantly fight for the right to reclaim my humanity and to just be. Each and every one of these names have been a heavy yoke on me, constraining my ability to blossom and forcing me to try to plead innocence in a world that condemned me from the very beginning.

As an intersex person, my body and my integrity have been objects of ruthless examination. I was submitted to 'corrective' surgeries that tried to change my anatomy to the standard gender binary during all of my childhood, which left physical and emotional scars that still hurt deep down in my heart. Growing up knowing that my body is seen as a mistake, something that needs to be 'fixed', was the main thing that fuelled my fight to reclaim my integrity and my right to exist.

On top of that, my existence as a racialised woman in a society that gives privilege only to the white and to the masculine has meant carrying the burden of multiple stereotypes and misconceptions that try to strip me of my humanity. I've been exoticised, hyper-sexualised and reduced to mere constructs that deny my individuality. Wandering this world under the perception of 'the other', the intruder, has demanded unbreakable strength to keep my dignity untouched in front of the accusatory looks and hurtful remarks that were always coming down like an avalanche.

And yet, despite the challenges, I had to face my new reality. Ripped out from my motherland by the violence and persecution and forced into a trip full of dangers and uncertainties, I have always been treated like a burden, like an outcast that was looking for privileges that weren't meant for her. The impossibility to find a decent job and have a stable life became the constant reminder of my vulnerability and the precariousness that defined my entire being, leaving me on the margins of a society that refused to take me in.

"You are black, don't wear make-up, don't dress up, don't dress nice, don't talk, don't show us what you have studied. You are intersexed. I can't help you, we can't do anything for you, you have nothing, you have it all, go, no, not here, out, no, not there either, eat from the floor, do as I say, bow your head, bow, bow..."

I keep getting ripped from my autonomy and my right to choose over my own body. My actual necessities and experiences are relegated in favour of an agenda that only tries to fit me inside binary categories.

And if you put being a black woman on top of that, the load becomes even heavier. My skin colour, my Caribbean descent, my physical features and my body converge into the focus of a stigma that put the label of 'undesirable' on me, that sees me as someone that doesn't belong, that "should go back to her country" or that should be content with whatever happens to her. Not even being in the 'here and now' I'm able to escape the prejudice and discrimination that marked my reality since the first day. I found myself being relegated to the borders, to the most hazardous and vulnerable spaces. My intersexual being and my race became unbreakable strongholds between me and a decent life, between me and my dreams and aspirations. I am seen as 'the other', the intruder that has to be happy with the crumbs that society wishes to throw at her. My physical and emotional pain, product of a childhood full of medical violence and an adulthood marked by the recurrent attempts to survive are relegated to a second plane in favour of a supposed 'equality' that does nothing but continue my condition of being disposable.

And yet, I refuse to accept this destiny. My existence on its own is an act of resistance, a challenge to the system that insists on denying me my humanity. I hold onto my dignity and my hopes, turning myself into a voice that refuses to be silenced. I grow from my determination and from my conviction in the fact that I deserve to live in this world. And through this growing I also find the strength to keep fighting, to keep drawing a path that, even though is devious, I know will lead to a horizon full of equality and inclusion.

I've learned to embrace the complexity of me, to find strength where everyone else sees weakness. I've discovered that my intersexuality is not a condition but a legitimate way of being alive, an expression of human diversity that deserves to be cherished. I've claimed my right to be a woman in my own terms without submitting to the standards imposed by a society that is always judging and rejecting me.

And I've hardened my resistance against all form of stereotyping or objectifying. My voice rises up like a sworn statement of my ability to blossom even in the toughest of conditions, a scream that refuses to be shut down or erased. Growing up in these circumstances forged me into an unsparing fighter, a survivor that holds onto her own worthiness and hopefulness even when this world seems determined to disclaim her right to exist.

> "My existence on its own is an act of resistance"

I know that my fight is not only mine but it also belongs to those who, like me, have been displaced to the borders. Even though my body has been the object of so much scrutiny and manipulation, even though my skin has been the reason for stigma and rejection, my spirit remains intact. With a braveness forged from adversity, I stand in front of the whole world and raise my voice to demand the licence I have over who I am with no shame or fear. Because intersexuality is not an identity or a gender, it is a natural biological variation that deserves to be celebrated and respected.

And even in the middle of this battle I yearn for a future where my existence is not something to fuss about or to reject, but to accept and value. I dream of the day I'll walk freely and with no fear, not having to justify myself or hide who I am. And in this way, with every step I take, with every story I share, my intersexual body blossoms as an act of stubborn resilience, defying the limits of what society thinks is "normal". Growing up in a world that insists on keeping us small is, in itself, a subversive act, is to take the reins of our own narratives and refashion the concept of humanity. I refuse to accept the labels, the diagnostics, the attempts to define me. I'm much more than that. I'm a constellation of possibilities, a symphony of variations, a canvas in constant evolution. By growing I amplify my existence and I turn into a beacon of hope to those who, like me, dare to defy the conventions and demand their rights to fully live as they are.

Joy is a new dress I haven't had the courage to put on yet

ITSH

I woke up in a pool of grief, at some point it wasn't new to me.
I splash my face in a mirror I can face now
without looking away, without turning my face down.
I grew power in the cracks of broken bones,
I told myself, "There's good soil under broken homes."
There is no narrative for me, my path was etched into a landscape that was not expecting company.

I looked for stories to relate to and found nothing,
Statuesque I felt convinced my chest contained no substance.
If there's no precedent for girls like me who make it long,
what was I to hold onto when my head shrouded up with fog?
I took it as a sign that I was just a flawed design.
Maybe I was onto something when I treat myself unkind.
But there's no length that I can stray where I outrun the day.
Every bruise and every mark is proof I'm tough to move.

I have become the harshest critic that exists,
and yet I survive my own fists, and I still wake, and I persist.
And once I've gone down every list of differences, and days I wish I didn't exist,
all that remains is my bright hair and these blue eyes and what I write.

The grip of fear around my neck will let up, I will make it sweat.
Those who doubt and those who gawk are powerless to stop what's next.

Grow through emotions

Ciara

Gender is over

Ranzie Orcena

"The existence of intersex people is proof that nature doesn't see gender as a binary."

- Dr. Colette Lord.

GENDER IS OVER

Art by: RMO

Me falta un cromosoma, me sobran ganas de vivir

Marel

Soy la menor de dos hermanas, nacida y criada al norte de México. Nací por parto natural, sin complicaciones y rápido. Sin embargo, nací con los pies y las manos hinchadas, así que los doctores decidieron esperar a que se me desinflamaran y, si no sucedía, le darían seguimiento. Como seguía igual, decidieron realizarme un cariotipo, el cual dio como resultado que mis cromosomas son X0, es decir, Síndrome de Turner. Esta condición la tiene 1 de cada 2500 niñas.

Ahí empezó el peregrinar en los hospitales. La genetista vigilaba mi crecimiento, y como estaba creciendo dentro de lo 'normal', nunca me administraron hormona de crecimiento. A mí me hubiera gustado crecer más, porque parte de mi familia mide 1.70 m o más, y yo no llegué a esa estatura.

Cuando tenía 9 años, desarrollé hipotiroidismo, que es característico del síndrome de Turner. Así que decidieron enviarme a endocrinología pediátrica. Me trató una endocrinóloga pediatra y dio seguimiento al hipotiroidismo, y a los 12 años empezó a administrarme estrógenos equinos y progesterona.

Como parte de las comorbilidades del síndrome de Turner, a los 13 años desarrollé linfedema de miembros inferiores. También tengo el riñón en herradura, lo que me hace propensa a infecciones urinarias. Actualmente estoy controlada de todo esto y llevo un seguimiento.

> "Desde que naciste estás en menopausia"

Después de que comencé con el tratamiento de estrógenos y progesterona, mi cuerpo comenzó a desarrollar características sexuales secundarias típicamente femeninas, también comencé con mi menstruación. Todo iba bien, pero aproximadamente a mis 15 años, me enteré que no podría tener hijos biológicos... la verdad eso me entristeció mucho, ya que una parte de mi anhelaba eso. Sin embargo, a mi corta edad, fui consciente de que jamás sucedería.

Pasó el tiempo, estudié dos licenciaturas y una maestría. A mis 25 años tuve mi primer empleo formal, e ingresé a un sistema en donde una de las prestaciones es el servicio médico. Así que empecé a atenderme a través de ese servicio médico.

Para entonces yo seguía tomando hormonas (estrógenos y progesterona) en diferentes presentaciones. Busqué ayuda para darle seguimiento a mi tratamiento hormonal, hasta que un ginecólogo me recetó hormonas bioidénticas. Compré estas hormonas y comencé el nuevo tratamiento. Sin embargo, al pasar un tiempo consumiéndolas, comencé con una secreción por el pezón, y, después de mucha insistencia de mi parte, me realizaron una biopsia y me informaron que tenía cáncer de mama resultado del tratamiento hormonal. Inmediatamente me retiraron las hormonas y me comenzaron a administrar un tratamiento con bloqueadores hormonales, además, me hicieron ganglio centinela y radioterapia.

En el transcurso del diagnóstico del cáncer, pasé por situaciones sumamente incómodas. Yo ya sabía que algo pasaba con mi cuerpo, y un ginecólogo que me estaba atendiendo me comentó que ya no consumiera las hormonas, a lo que yo le respondí que si no las consumía me llegaría la menopausia, y él me dijo: "Desde que naciste estás en menopausia". Comentario que me pareció sumamente denigrante e innecesario. Este mismo ginecólogo no quería operarme, a pesar de que su jefe le mandó un escrito diciéndole que realizara protocolo por mastopatía. Así que tuve que quejarme, me cambiaron de ginecólogo, y posteriormente me intervinieron y continué el tratamiento.

Cuando estaba atravesando todo esto, recibí diversos comentarios de parte de familiares, como: "Qué bueno que tu enfermaste de cáncer y no tu hermana, porque ella tiene hijos", este tipo de comentarios realmente me dolieron y pienso que son denigrantes. Así mismo, hace poco falleció una amiga de mi edad, ella no tuvo hijos, y escuché comentarios como: "¡Qué bueno que no tuvo hijos!". Entiendo que al morir no dejó en la orfandad a nadie... sin embargo, la vida de toda persona es igual de importante independientemente de si tienes la capacidad de engendrar vida o no. También considero que lo verdaderamente importante es darle una buena calidad de vida a los hijos que se tienen, cosa que muchas personas que se dicen padres o madres, no hacen.

Finalmente logré recuperarme y vencer el cáncer de mama. A pesar de todas las complicaciones e implicaciones, siempre he salido adelante. Actualmente, tengo un trabajo estable, gracias al cual mis padres y yo tenemos servicio médico, pude adquirir mi patrimonio y soy autosuficiente.

Ahora, me gustaría retomar y contar mi historia más detalladamente en cuanto a la intersexualidad. Yo siempre me identifiqué como mujer y me gustan los varones.

Sin embargo, siempre supe que algo pasaba conmigo, algo que no sabía cómo podía explicar. En el 2022 asistí a una conferencia y ahí escuché el término intersexualidad, y vi que las personas con Turner son intersexuales. Eso me generó sentimientos encontrados, por una parte sentí angustia, pero por otra alivio, porque pude saber que yo era una mujer intersexual, y que mis particularidades me hacen única, irrepetible y una sobreviviente.

"la vida de toda persona es igual de importante"

Escribo este relato para visibilizar el síndrome de Turner, para tener cuidado con el tratamiento hormonal y sus implicaciones en la salud, y para contribuir a que realmente exista un protocolo y seguimiento médico adecuados. Estoy consciente que todos los casos son diferentes, sin embargo, la atención médica debe ser digna, adecuada y oportuna. A su vez quiero externar que es de suma importancia contar con el respaldo de un diagnóstico mediante un cariotipo, ya que en mi caso mis papás nunca tuvieron la precaución de pedirlo y resguardarlo.

También quiero visibilizar la importancia de que las personas con Turner tengamos el derecho a una atención médica gratuita y digna de por vida, así como a los estudios y a un tratamiento médico adecuado e informado, ya que no todas las personas contamos con acceso a un sistema de salud realmente digno. A su vez, pienso que es de suma importancia la detección oportuna. Mis padres tampoco previeron y no tuvieron la precaución de procurar un buen servicio médico y vitalicio para mi atención, y cuando cumplí 21 años me quitaron automáticamente el seguro social.

Actualmente, gracias a mi trabajo, tengo acceso a servicio médico, pero, considero de suma importancia el gestionar que este sea un derecho y una garantía inherente que se brinde a las personas con Turner, porque como yo, hay muchas mujeres que pasan por situaciones similares.

Ahora sé que no estoy sola, que existe mucha gente que realmente me ha ayudado, sé dónde pedir ayuda y cómo, y también sé cuándo debo de alzar la voz cuando algo no está bien y los medios adecuados para hacerlo.

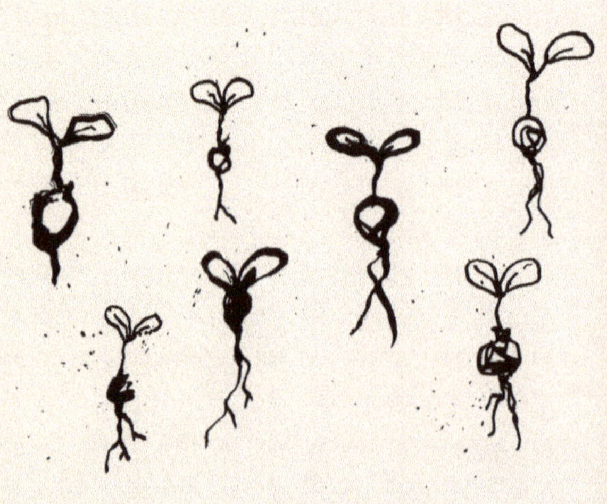

I'm missing a chromosome, but I have plenty of desire to live

Marel

I am the youngest of two sisters, born and raised in northern Mexico. I was born through a natural birth, without complications and quickly. However, I was born with swollen hands and feet, so the doctors decided to wait for the swelling to go down and, if it didn't, they would follow up. As the swelling persisted, they decided to perform a karyotype test, which revealed that my chromosomes are XO, that is, Turner Syndrome. This condition affects 1 in every 2500 girls.

> "You've been in menopause since you were born"

That's when my journey through hospitals began. The geneticist monitored my growth, and since I was growing within the 'normal' range, I was never administered growth hormone. I would have liked to grow taller because part of my family is 1.70 metres or taller. I didn't reach that height.

When I was 9 years old, I developed hypothyroidism, which is characteristic of Turner Syndrome. So, they decided to send me to paediatric endocrinology. The paediatric endocrinologist treated my hypothyroidism and, at age 12, she started giving me equine estrogens and progesterone.

As part of the comorbidities of Turner Syndrome, at 13, I developed lymphedema in my lower limbs. I also have a horseshoe kidney, which makes me prone to urinary infections. Currently, all of this is under control, and I am being monitored.

After starting the treatment with estrogens and progesterone, my body began to develop typically female secondary sex characteristics. I also started menstruating.

Everything was going well, but around the age of 15, I found out that I wouldn't be able to have biological children...this really saddened me, as part of me longed for that. However, at my young age, I was aware that it would never happen.

Time passed, I studied two bachelor's degrees and a master's degree. At 25, I had my first formal job, and I joined a system where one of the benefits is health insurance. So, I started getting treatment through that health insurance.

By then, I was still taking hormones—estrogens and progesterone—in different forms. I sought help to follow up on my hormonal treatment until a gynaecologist prescribed bioidentical hormones. I bought these hormones and started the new treatment. However, after some time consuming this treatment, I began to have nipple discharge, and after I insisted a lot, they performed a biopsy. I was informed that I had breast cancer because of the hormonal treatment. The hormones were immediately withdrawn, and I began treatment with hormone blockers, underwent sentinel node biopsy, and had radiotherapy.

During the cancer diagnosis process, I went through extremely uncomfortable situations. I already knew something was happening with my body, and a gynaecologist who was treating me told me to stop taking the hormones, to which I responded that if I didn't take them, I would go through menopause, and he said to me: "You've been in menopause since you were born". I found this comment extremely degrading and unnecessary. This same gynaecologist didn't want to operate on me, despite his boss sending him a written order to perform a protocol for mastopathy. So, I had to complain. I was assigned a different gynaecologist, and subsequently, I had the surgery and continued the treatment.

While going through all of this, I received various comments from family members, such as: "It's good that you got cancer and not your sister because she has children," which really hurt me, and I think is degrading. Similarly, recently a friend of my age passed away; she did not have children, and I heard comments like: "It's good she didn't have children!" I understand that by dying, she didn't leave anyone orphaned, however the life of every person is equally important, regardless of whether you have children or not. I also believe that what truly matters is giving a good quality of life to the children one has, something many people who call themselves parents do not do.

I finally managed to recover and beat breast cancer. Despite all the complications and implications, I have always moved forward. Currently, I have a stable job, thanks to which my parents and I have health insurance, I was able to acquire my own assets, and I am self-sufficient.

Now, I would like to go back and tell my story in more detail regarding intersex. I have always identified as a woman and I like men. However, I always knew something was different about me, something I didn't know how to explain.

In 2022, I attended a conference and heard the term intersex, and I noticed that people with Turner Syndrome are intersex. This generated mixed feelings in me; on the one hand, I felt anguish, but on the other hand, relief, because I was able to know that I was an intersex woman, and that my particularities make me unique, unrepeatable, and a survivor.

"the life of every person is equally important"

I write this story to raise awareness about Turner Syndrome, to be cautious with hormonal treatment and its implications for health, and to contribute to the existence of an adequate medical protocol and follow-up. I am aware that all cases are different; however, medical care must be dignified, adequate, and timely. Additionally, I want to emphasise the importance of having the support of a diagnosis through a karyotype, as in my case my parents never had the foresight to request and preserve it.

I also want to highlight the importance of people with Turner Syndrome having the right to dignified and free medical care for life, as well as access to their medical records and appropriate and informed medical treatment, since not everyone has access to a truly dignified health system. Moreover, I believe that early detection is crucial. My parents also did not foresee or take the precaution of providing good and lifelong medical service for my care, and when I turned 21, my health insurance was automatically taken away.

Currently, thanks to my job, I have access to a health insurance, but I consider it extremely important to ensure that this is an inherent right and guarantee provided to people with Turner Syndrome, because, like me, many women go through similar situations.

Now I know that I am not alone, that there are many people who have truly helped me. I know where and how to ask for help, and I also know when to raise my voice when something is not right, and the appropriate means to do so.

Together we bloom

Kon Zer

How beautiful is growth!

Growth means being scared but not letting that fear rule you.
Growth is when the constant feeling of uncertainty starts to fade away, making space for a newfound sense of confidence.
Growth is to begin trusting again, both others and yourself, valuing your voice, and listening to your own needs.
Growth is to reclaim the reins of your life, making decisions based on your own needs and aspirations.
Growth is no longer fearing growth, to be untroubled by change for the better.
Growth is to overcome obstacles, whether self-imposed or thrown your way by others, rediscovering happiness in your life and starting to live happily again.

Τι ωραία που είναι η εξέλιξη!

Εξέλιξη είναι να φοβόσουν αλλά να μην φοβάσαι πια.
Εξέλιξη είναι όταν το συνεχές αίσθημα της αβεβαιότητας σιγά σιγά φεύγει, αφήνοντας χώρο για ένα νέο αίσθημα σιγουριάς και αυτοπεποίθησης.
Εξελιξη είναι να αρχίζεις να εμπιστεύεσαι πάλι τους γύρω σου αλλά και τον εαυτό σου, να του δίνεις σημασία, να τον ακούς και να τον υπολογίζεις.
Εξέλιξη είναι να παίρνεις πάλι τα ινία της ζωής σου, να παιρνεις αποφάσεις βασισμένες στις δικές σου ανάγκες και προσδοκίες.
Εξέλιξη είναι να μην φοβάσαι πια την εξέλιξη, να μην σε αγχώνει η αλλαγή προς το καλύτερο.
Εξέλιξη είναι να ξεπερασεις τα εμπόδια που είτε εσύ ο ίδιος είτε οι άλλοι έβαλαν στον δρόμο σου και να αρχίσεις να ζεις τη ζωή σου ευτυχισμένος ξανά.

Isn't growth beautiful?

This collage contains snapshots that mark milestones in my personal journey of growth. Moments in which I felt the transformation from a girl who hid and feared to speak or visit her doctor, to a woman who steps out, speaks up, supports her community and asserts her rights. This journey is vast and never-ending, but also incredibly rewarding, filled with challenges and victories. Remember, your journey of growth is unique to you, but you're never alone. We are like flowers whose growth may not always flourish, but together, we can blossom. So, keep looking ahead, because that's where your journey is leading you.

Ωραία δεν είναι η εξέλιξη;

Το κολαζ αυτό περιέχει στιγμιότυπα που αποτελούν ορόσημα στο ταξίδι της δικής μου εξέλιξης. Στιγμές που ένιωσα την αλλαγή από ένα κορίτσι που κρυβόταν και φοβόταν να μιλήσει ή να πάει στον γιατρό του, σε μια γυναίκα που βγαίνει έξω και μιλάει στηρίζοντας την κοινότητα της και διεκδικόντας τα δικαιώματα της.
Το ταξίδι αυτό είναι μεγάλο και δεν σταματάει ποτέ, εύχομαι όλοι όμως να έχουμε στιγμές που συνειδητοποιούμε αυτήν την εξέλιξη, το σημείο που έχουμε φτάσει αλλά και το που μπορούμε να φτάσουμε. Είμαστε σαν λουλούδια που η ανάπτυξη τους μπορεί να μην ευδοκιμεί πάντα αλλά μαζί μπορούμε να ανθίσουμε.

Fut—
Lego mis favoritos

Vanessy

Soccer — Lego my favourites
Character 1: I've played soccer and LEGO all my life, I can't miss.

Character 2: I'm the best at this, ahhh!

Soccer—
Lego my favourites

My intersex flag

Nico

Inusual

Free

Dos,
tenía solo dos años
cuando un misterioso interruptor se activó:
crecimiento del clítoris, sexo indefinido;
vello púbico, cambio adolescente,
crecimiento, gran estirón;
pubertad es la palabra,
inusual, el atributo.

Tres,
tenía solo tres años
cuando una nube negra invadió mi mente,
me preguntaba qué era en realidad:
¿un niño, una niña o algo más?
Contemplando el arbusto bajo mis pantalones,
con tan solo tres años,
me preguntaba qué era eso en realidad.

Cuatro,
tenía solo cuatro años
cuando mis hormonas tuvieron su primera fiesta.
Una llama abrasadora, furia hormonal,
invadió mi cuerpo
y me invitó a darme amor
y a florecer en una nueva manera.

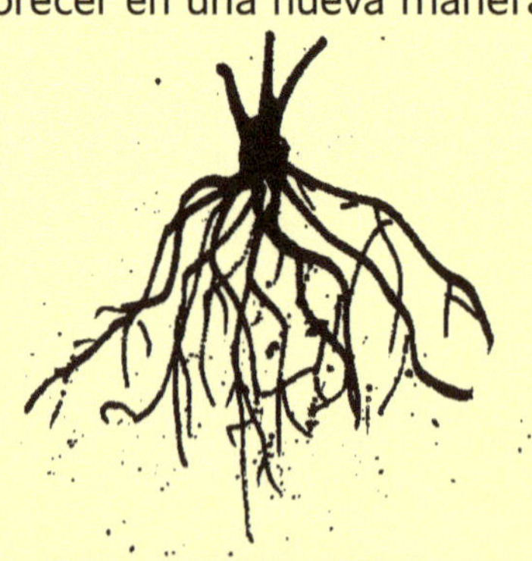

Los años pasaron
y seguí creciendo,
cambiando, preguntándome y amándome;
pero de pronto el interruptor se apagó
y la niña más alta del jardín
se convirtió en la más bajita de la primaria.
Entonces, seguí preguntándome
qué, por qué y cómo.
Mi cuerpo dejó de crecer
pero yo seguí floreciendo.

Crecí
pensando que no había nadie en el mundo
como yo,
que era la única
con características sexuales peculiares.
Estaba confundida y dudosa acerca de mi sexo.

Catorce,
tenía catorce años cuando conocí a alguien
como yo.
Entonces comprendí
que no estaba sola.

Quince,
tenía quince años cuando
mi novio me enseñó
que no había nada malo en mí.
Entonces dejé de ser un monstruo
para convertirme en flor.

Unusual

Free

Two,
I was only two
when a mysterious switch turned on:
clit grew up, undefined sex;
pubic hair, teenage change;
growth, big spurt;
puberty is the noun,
unusual, the attribute.

Three,
I was only three
when a black cloud took my mind,
wondering what I really was:
a boy, a girl, or something else?
Looking at the bush under my pants,
I was only three,
wondering what it actually was.

Four,
I was only four
when my hormones had their first party.
A burning flame, hormone rage,
took my body
and invited me to love myself
and bloom in a new way.

Years went by
and I kept growing,
changing, wondering and loving;
but suddenly, the switch turned off
and the tallest girl in kindergarten
became the shortest
in primary school.
Then I kept wondering
what, why and how.
My body stopped growing
but I kept blooming.

I grew up
thinking that there was nobody
in the world
like me,
that I was the only one
with peculiar sex characteristics.
I was confused and doubtful
about my sex.

Fourteen,
I was fourteen when I met someone
like me.
I understood then
that I wasn't the only one.

Fifteen,
I was fifteen when
my boyfriend taught me
that there was nothing wrong
with me.
I stopped being a monster
and bloomed into a flower.

Crecer juntos

Ayito

Growing together

Existen personas Intersex, que también son trans

Ayito

There are intersex people who are also trans

From Shubhra to Noor-Alom: My Journey of Resilience and Empowerment

Noor Alom

Hello, my name is Noor Alom. I am an intersex individual and I was born as Shubhra. Today, I want to share my journey from Shubhra to Noor Alom, a story of resilience, transformation, and hope.

I was born into a noble Muslim family in Savar, a bustling city near Dhaka, the capital of Bangladesh. From the very beginning, my life was marked by neglect and misunderstanding from both my family and society. My birth was not celebrated; instead, it was met with confusion and dismay because I was not distinctly identified as either a boy or a girl. This ambiguity led to a childhood filled with pain and a quest for a clear gender identity.

In the first six years of my life, I underwent six surgeries as my family and doctors tried to assign me a gender. After the first four surgeries, the doctors decided I was a girl, and my family began raising me as one. Two years later, after two more surgeries, the doctors reversed their decision, declaring I was a boy. Thus, the first nine years of my life were a tumultuous journey of medical interventions and shifting identities.

On the advice of doctors and a local cleric, I was renamed Noor Alom and enrolled in a boys' school. However, adolescence brought more challenges. As I developed breasts, I faced severe bullying and was eventually expelled from school. The harsh words and relentless bullying from my peers and the wider community forced me to end my formal education prematurely.

Even within my own family, I was hidden and treated with shame. My family kept my existence a secret, so much so that my aunt only discovered I existed 19 years after her marriage. The stigma of my intersex identity even affected my siblings' marital prospects, leading to multiple broken engagements.

Despair overwhelmed me, and I attempted suicide several times. Eventually, unable to bear the neglect and humiliation any longer, I left home. I wandered from door to door in search of a job but found no refuge until I was taken in by a Hijra community. However, even there, life was not easy, and I returned to my family with great difficulty.

Despite the endless contempt and humiliation from my family and society, I refused to give up. I had an indomitable spirit and vowed to stand on my own feet and contribute positively to society. Today, I am a successful entrepreneur. I run a thriving food cart near the Savar police station, where I sell delicious food daily.

"Even within my own family, I was hidden and treated with shame."

But my journey didn't end with personal success. I wanted to ensure that others like me wouldn't have to endure the same struggles alone. I founded an organisation called 'Intersex Bangladesh', dedicated to advocating for the rights and health of intersex individuals. Intersex Bangladesh works tirelessly for the skill development and training of intersex people, empowering them to lead dignified and independent lives.

Through 'Intersex Bangladesh', we are creating a community where intersex individuals are respected, understood, and supported. We provide essential services, education, and training, helping intersex people build their skills and achieve their dreams.

My story is one of resilience and hope. From the neglect and pain of my early years, I have emerged stronger and more determined to make a difference. I am Noor Alom, and I am here to tell you that no matter how difficult the journey, it is possible to rise above the challenges and create a better future for ourselves and others. Let us stand together, support each other, and work towards a society where everyone, regardless of their gender identity, is respected and valued.

Crecer

Azucena

Un jueves del mes de febrero de 1991, en la ciudad de Los Mochis, Sinaloa, nació una niña. Así lo declaró el médico ginecólogo a la mamá de la bebé, quien tenía el gran anhelo de tener entre sus brazos a una parte de su vida, su primer amor, a quien cuidaría con todo su ser ante cualquier adversidad. Al nacer, la niña fue sometida a los estudios de rutina en pediatría para detectar posibles problemas que podría desarrollar a lo largo de su vida, además de recibir las vacunas correspondientes. Días después del nacimiento, tanto la menor como su madre fueron dadas de alta del hospital y se trasladaron en un carro particular a su pueblo de origen, donde la madre llevaba entre sus brazos a su adoración.

Todo marchaba con normalidad. La mamá de la menor menciona que nunca notó nada fuera de lo normal en la salud de su infante. Con el apoyo de su padre, el abuelo de la menor, de nombre Emeterio, quien inicialmente menospreciaba a la niña e incluso hacía comentarios discriminatorios sobre su tono de piel más oscuro, aludiendo a que la mamá tenía un tono de piel más blanco y su bebé era de piel morena. También hacía comentarios en contra del padre, lo que hacía sentir mal a la madre. En un momento en el que necesitaba sentir el respaldo de su familia, solo recibía comentarios que le ocasionaban tristeza.

> "Que necesitaba sentir el respaldo de su familia"

El padre nunca se hizo cargo de los gastos que conlleva el tener un infante, así que la responsabilidad recaía sobre la madre de la menor de nombre Doris, quien nombró a su hija Azucena. En sus primeros años de vida, el abuelo materno se hizo cargo de los gastos, a pesar de los comentarios discriminatorios que constantemente dirigía a Doris y a Azucena. Cuando Azucena apenas tenía 3 años de edad, Doris, con valentía, decidió comenzar a trabajar en una empresa que procesaba jitomates, los hacía puré y los envasaba para su venta. La empresa también procesaba chiles en lata y otras verduras. Cuando Doris tomó la decisión de trabajar en la empresa, habló con su padre, Emeterio, porque era la única persona que podía apoyarla con la crianza de Azucena, y cuidarla mientras ella trabajaba. La mamá de Doris había fallecido cuando ella apenas tenía 19 años.

Con el tiempo, Emeterio comenzó a sentir amor por su nieta Azucena y dejó de importarle su color de piel o quién era su padre. Emeterio sentía que debía proteger a su nieta y apoyar a su hija Doris en lo que estuviera en sus posibilidades. Incluso llegó a advertir a sus otros nietos que no toleraría que maltratasen a Azucena.

Un día, cuando Azucena tenía 8 años, se encontraba en el baño. Su madre abrió la puerta y notó algo inusual en sus genitales. Tras consultar con su hermano de confianza, decidieron llevar a Azucena al médico, y, tiempo después, fue diagnosticada con hiperplasia suprarrenal congénita.

Durante su niñez y adolescencia, Azucena creció sintiéndose diferente a las demás niñas. Era habitual que enfrentara discriminación por su apariencia, por el tono de su voz y por su comportamiento.

"Anteriormente tímida y temerosa, ahora es una persona valiente"

Sin embargo, hoy en día, Azucena es una persona que ha sabido enfrentar situaciones muy complejas. Cuando escucha comentarios negativos sobre su persona, los enfrenta sin temor. Anteriormente tímida y temerosa, ahora es una persona valiente, que no agacha la mirada y que simplemente ignora los comentarios de las personas que intentan hacerla sentir mal. Ella sabe que la juzgan sin conocerla y que son personas que solo se basan en las apariencias.

"Se feliz porque solo se vive una vez."

Growing up

Azucena

One Thursday in February 1991, in the city of Los Mochis, Sinaloa, a baby girl was born. This was declared by the gynaecologist to the baby's mother, who had a great desire to have her daughter, her first love, in her arms, whom she would protect with all her being against any adversity. At birth, the girl underwent routine paediatric exams to detect any possible problems that might develop throughout her life, in addition to receiving the corresponding vaccines. Days after the birth, both the baby and her mother were discharged from the hospital and travelled in a private car to their hometown, where the mother carried her beloved in her arms.

Everything seemed 'normal', and the girl's mother mentioned that she never noticed anything unusual in her infant's health. With the support of her father, the child's grandfather named Emeterio, who initially belittled the child and even made discriminatory comments about her darker skin tone, alluding to the fact that the mother had lighter skin while the baby was brown-skinned. He also made derogatory comments about the father, which made the mother feel bad. At a time when she needed to feel the support of her family, she only received comments that made her sad.

"She needed to feel the support of her family"

The father never took responsibility for the expenses that come with having a child, so the responsibility fell on the girl's mother, named Doris, who named her daughter Azucena. In her early years, the maternal grandfather covered the expenses, despite the discriminatory comments he constantly directed at Doris and Azucena. When Azucena was just 3 years old, Doris bravely decided to start working at a company that processed tomatoes into puree and canned them for sale; the company also canned chillies and other vegetables. When Doris decided to work at the company, she spoke to her father, Emeterio, because he was the only person who could help her with raising Azucena and take care of her while she worked. Doris's mother had died when she was only 19 years old.

Over time, Emeterio began to feel love for his granddaughter Azucena, and he no longer cared about her skin colour or who her father was. Emeterio felt he had to protect his granddaughter and support his daughter Doris in whatever way he could. He even warned his other grandchildren that he would not tolerate them mistreating Azucena.

One day, when Azucena was 8 years old, she was in the bathroom. Her mother opened the door and noticed something unusual about her genitals. After consulting with her trusted brother, they decided to take Azucena to the doctor, and later, she was diagnosed with congenital adrenal hyperplasia.

During her childhood and adolescence, Azucena grew up feeling different from other girls. She often faced discrimination because of her appearance, her voice tone, and her behaviour.

“Once shy and fearful, she is now a brave person”

However, today, Azucena is a person who has learned to face the complex situations she has encountered. When she hears negative comments about herself, she confronts them without fear. Once shy and fearful, she is now a brave person who does not lower her gaze and simply ignores the comments of people who try to make her feel bad. She knows they judge her without knowing her and that they are people who only judge based on appearances.

“Be happy because you only live once.”

CHANGE
YOUR
HEARTS
NOT OUR
PARTS

Inbetween

Juniper Fox

I was full of hatred,
because of how I was treated.
Only my pain understood who I was.
I used to dam the line that split me in half,
creating two sides
I didn't know I had.
I know it's a part of me—
something to love, something new,
something to learn from,
and hopefully they'll learn it too.

Stuck in-between,
getting to know my better halves.
Used to be afraid—
It wasn't a phase.
All their hate, twisted into words,
tied down by fate.

I was meant to know
when I needed it the most.
It was painful
being a part of this world.
Stripped of my voice,
I didn't get a say,
didn't have a choice,
in the part I wanted to play.

You said to me,
"I know identity is hard for you,
because of everything you've been through,
trapped in and closeted from your truth.

But who really knows you,
better than you know yourself?
You are judged for being who you are,
hated for who you are not,
don't know who you will become,
But don't worry, they are just words
Not a measure of everything you already are."

I've unlocked more of my brain,
more potential.
I'm not an experiment,
waiting for your table.
I am not your latest temptation,
your latest accomplishment.
I am not the story in your head,
being told as a fable
because...surprise,
I exist.

I wasn't ready to let go of the person I thought I was,
because I felt something different woven in my soul,
I was already set in stone,
a story written, ready to be told.
It's a part of me—
something to love, something new,
something to learn from,
and hopefully they'll learn it too.

Surviving

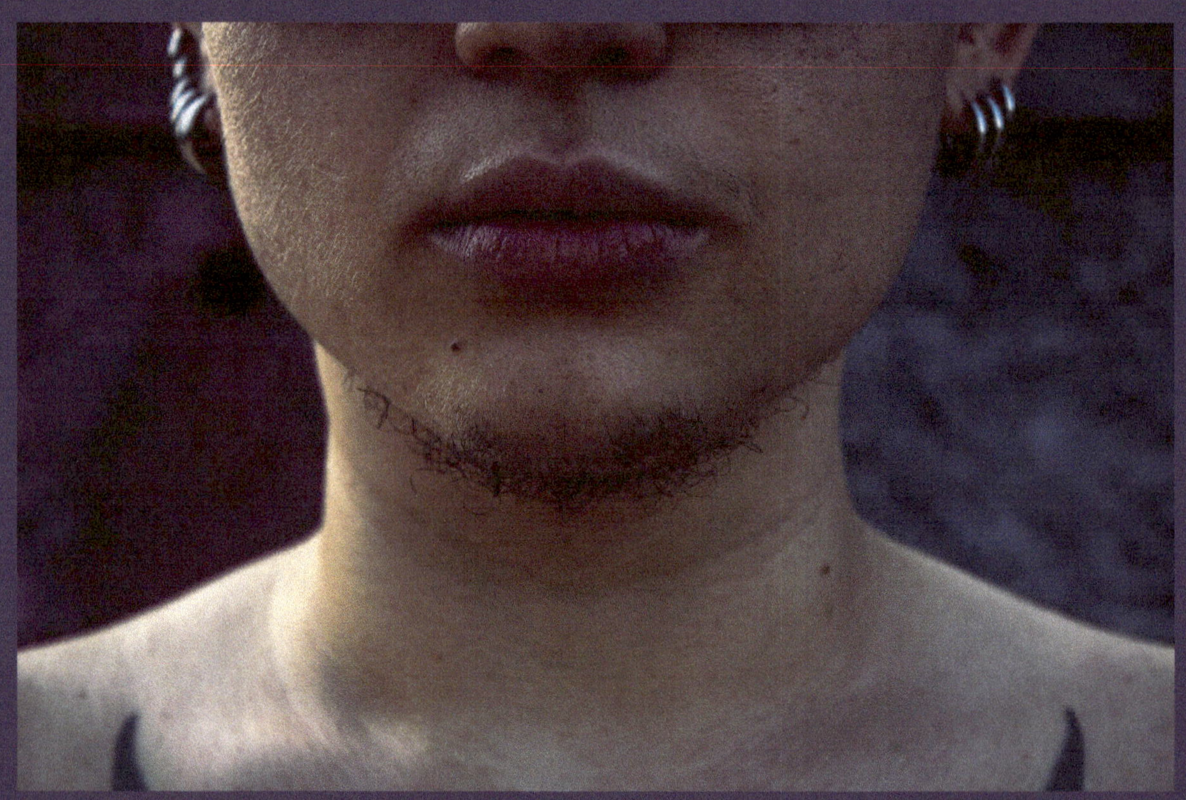

Mel Kurutta

Healing

Mel Kurutta

Censurable

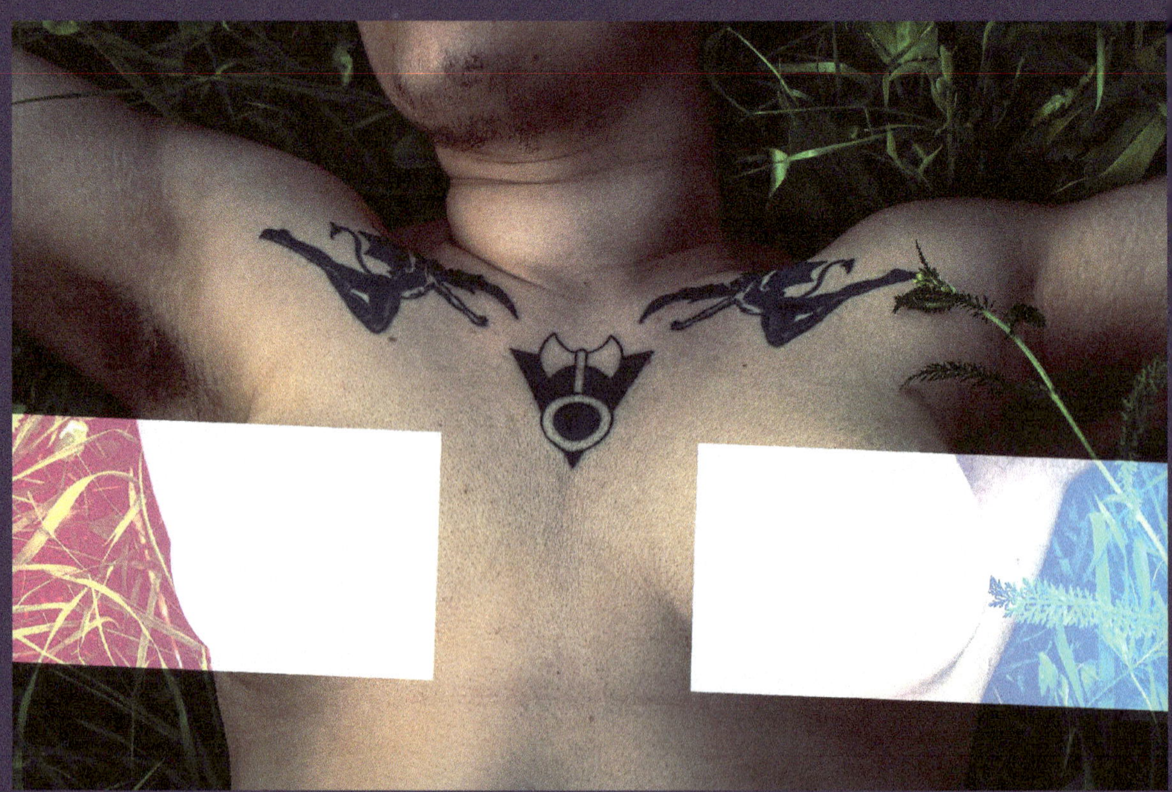

Mel Kurutta

Per me, crescere significa accettare tutte le conseguenze delle mie azioni. Accetto il corpo [intersex] in cui vivo, considerato uno scherzo della natura: lo amo e me ne prendo cura, ogni giorno di più. Lo vivo nella sua interezza, nonostante le difficoltà sociali che comporta.

For me, growing up means accepting all the consequences of my actions. I embrace the [intersex] body I live in, which is considered a freak of nature: I love it and take care of it, every day more and more. I live it in its wholeness, despite the social difficulties it involves.

Evolución

Yela

Siempre se ha dicho que el pasado debe quedar en el pasado, también hay un dicho que dice: "para atrás ni para tomar impulso". Pero muchas veces es necesario darle un vistazo a esa vida que quedó atrás, a esos momentos que superamos y nos ayudaron a ser las personas que somos ahora. Yo recuerdo que siempre fui una persona introvertida, sumisa, temerosa, sin sueños. Nunca pensaba en mi futuro, me sentía tan extraña en este mundo que sentía que no pertenecía a ningún lugar.

El desprecio que me dirigían otras personas, muchas veces hizo que me autocastigara y me despreciara a mí misma. Siendo sincera, muchas veces me cuesta creer todo lo que tuve que superar. Solo existe un factor y es que nunca me rendí a pesar del dolor, de la vergüenza, del daño que me hacían otras personas. Sin importar todo esto salía a estudiar, a trabajar.

Las ganas de investigar y de querer saber porque mi cuerpo era diferente, porque no podía encajar... esa curiosidad me llevó hasta Brújula intersexual y nunca me cansaré de darles las gracias, pues ahí encontré todo lo que necesitaba para encontrar las respuestas que necesitaba. Esa brújula me indicó cuál era el camino.

Hoy soy una mujer segura, que sale a la calle con la frente en alto, las miradas curiosas ya no me lastiman y las preguntas imprudentes ya no me incomodan. Tengo una pareja que me complementa, que me ama y amo con todo mi corazón. Tengo un hogar, un empleo donde soy respetada. Tengo metas para mi crecimiento personal y también quiero seguir trabajando en el activismo intersexual y lograr que nuestras voces sean escuchadas.

"El desprecio que me dirigían otras personas, muchas veces hizo que me autocastigara y me despreciara a mí misma."

Esta es una lucha en la que no podemos rendirnos. Si no me rendí antes cuando estaba sola, no lo haré ahora que cuento con una comunidad. Solo cuando la oruga creyó que el mundo terminaba, se transformó en mariposa.

Evolution

Yela

It has always been said that the past should remain in the past, and there's also a saying: "Don't look back, not even to gain momentum." But often it's necessary to glance at the life that has passed, at those moments we overcame that helped us become who we are now. I remember I was always an introverted, submissive, fearful person with no dreams. I never thought about my future; I felt so out of place in this world that I felt I didn't belong anywhere.

The disdain from others often led me to self-punish and despise myself. To be honest, it's hard for me to believe everything I had to overcome. The only factor is that I never gave up despite the pain, the embarrassment, and the harm caused by others. Regardless of all this, I went out to study and work.

"The disdain from others often led me to self-punish and despise myself."

The desire to investigate and understand why my body was different, why I couldn't fit in... that curiosity led me to Brújula Intersexual, and I will never tire of thanking them because there I found everything I needed to get the answers I sought. That compass showed me the way.

Today I am a confident woman who walks the streets with her head held high. The curious gazes no longer hurt me, and the intrusive questions no longer make me uncomfortable. I have a partner who complements me, who loves me and whom I love with all my heart. I have a home and a job where I am respected. I have goals for my personal growth and I also want to continue working in intersex activism to ensure our voices are heard.

This is a struggle in which we cannot give up. If I didn't give up before when I was alone, I won't now that I have a community. Only when the caterpillar thought the world was over did it transform into a butterfly.

R. U
I KNO

Grow

Lee

It has never been easy growing up being intersex.
From the discrimination and bullying in school, to the hurtful words from relatives and all sorts of name-calling from society.

One day, as I was sitting in the morning enjoying the view of the sun, I looked up and saw a group of birds flying and they were making a shape like a circle. My mind began to wonder about how these birds survive—they are not employed by any company neither do they have credit cards—yet they feed and are able to fly and play around in the air freely without worrying about what those who are below are going to say or try to do.

That is the moment I was inspired that worrying will not solve any of my troubles. Rather, I need to have a mentality like that of a bird, enjoying every moment as it comes and be happy each day despite what anyone was going to say about me. I immediately stood up and spread my hands like the wings of a bird. I told myself that I refuse to be looked down upon and I will continue to rise despite what they say or try to do.

Since then, my self-esteem has grown and if I ever feel down, I look for a group of birds to feel motivated. I look forward to remaining in such high spirits and I remain hopeful that one day I will motivate others through this encounter I had with birds. I also look forward to be able to buy a house of my own someday and keep a few birds as pets so that I can wake up each morning and be motivated.

"I need to have a mentality like that of a bird, enjoying every moment as it comes"

STOP
You can
change
the world
at any time
at any time

Baby teeth

ITSH

Going 110 miles on the way to Grand River, a boy smiles at the thought of a sister.
The doctor rushes you into that sterile room with instruments to bring your child soon.
The pain is too much to describe, but nothing good in life comes without pain and time.
After hours of distress, you look down at your child and the pain just fades to happiness.

Chubby little fingers grip you, scared of what's to come.
You soothe the child; reassure them they will face no harm.
You will keep them safe, that's your sacred oath.
You've done it once before; you love what scares you most.

The doctor looks at clipboards and simply shakes his head.
"There's something wrong," he says.
You can't believe it, your child's safe asleep,
born on time with all their baby teeth.

He's the one with the degree.
He says the baby can be fixed, but it won't be cheap.
You'd do anything for your baby girl, so you let her go.

Minutes turn to hours as your mind begins to pace.
You ask another nurse who quickly turns away her face.
For hours there is no one strong enough to tell the truth.
Until the doctor's back.
"There was a complication, there was nothing we could do."

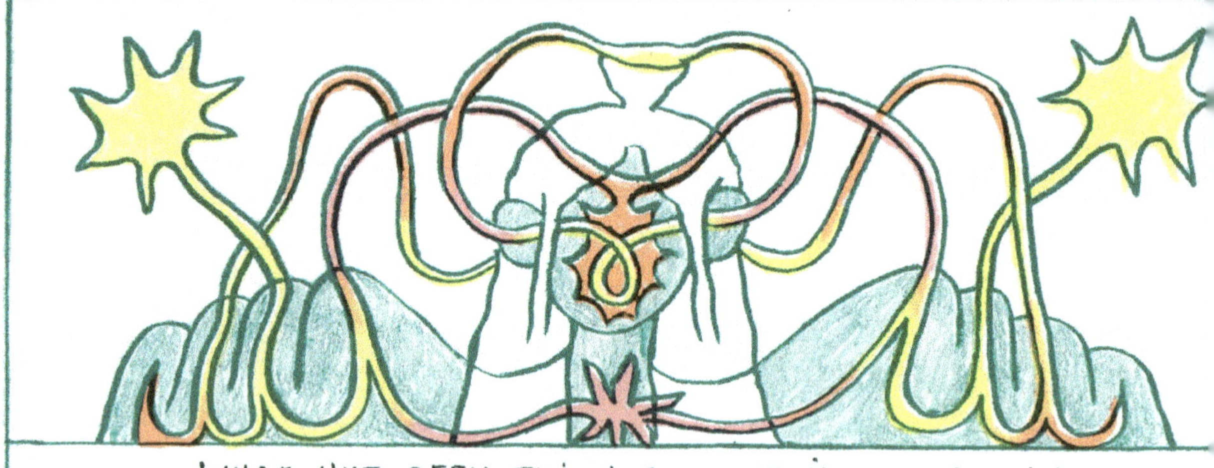

WHAT I'VE BEEN THINKING ABOUT INTERSEXUALITY

IS AN UNPOPULAR OPINION

PEOPLE DON'T LIKE THESE IDEAS

BUT I DON'T CARE, I'M GOING TO SAY WHAT I THINK.

AO

Otto Etraud & Kali

I FELT MUCH MORE CONNECTED TO THAT
STORY AND THAT NAME, MUCH MORE THAN
THE WORD INTERSEX, WHICH IS A
RATHER COLD MEDICAL TERM.
I CONNECTED WITH THAT PERSON WHO, ALTHOUGH THEY MAY NOT HAVE EXISTED,
I FELT REPRESENTED MANY PEOPLE WHO SURELY MUST HAVE EXISTED. BECAUSE THAT
DIDN'T COME FROM IMAGINATION, BUT
FROM REAL BEINGS WHO NEEDED AN
EXPLANATION. THAT PLACE WAS MYTH.

THEN, WITH THAT WORD, PEOPLE WERE DESIGNATED THROUGHOUT WESTERN HISTORY. IN THE
REST OF THE WORLD, I HAVE NO IDEA WHAT
HAPPENED. WHITEWASHING, COLONIZATION?
WELL, YES, I HAVE NO DOUBT, BUT I
FELT THAT SOMEHOW ONE COULD FORM A KIND OF CONSTELLATION, WHICH IN
THE END, I BELIEVE IS THE MOST IMPORTANT THING ABOUT THE TERM
INTERSEX.

IT'S THE REASON WHY I'M INTERESTED
IN BEING VISIBLE OR HEARD.
NOT JUST FOR DENOUNCING AND RECLAIM-
ING THE BRUTALITIES WE'VE LIVED THROUGH
BUT WITH THE POWER TO TRACE THE MISSING PARTS OF THE FAMILY TO CONSTE-
LLATE, SO OTHER PEOPLE CAN FEEL
THEY'RE PART OF SOMETHING,
AND NO LONGER BE IN SOLITUDE.

BELIEVE HERMAPHRODITUS HAS BEEN BORN THOUSANDS OF TIMES, AND WILL CON-
TINUE TO BE BORN UNTIL THE WORLD SOMEDAY UNDERSTANDS AND WELCOMES THEM.

AND THEY CEASE TO BE A MYTHICAL BEING, AND WE EVEN STOP HAVING NAME

AND EVEN THE NAMES HERMAPHRODITUS AND INTERSEX ARE FORGOTTE

AND WE NO LONGER HAVE MEMORY OF THAT MYTH, BECAUSE IT'S SIMPLY

LONGER NEEDED, NEITHER HERE, NOR WHERE YOU ARE, NOR ANYWHERE

I find myself in flowers

Mouse

I get my first job in a flower shop by accident. I have to choose something for work experience, and the book I'm hiding in features characters opening one, so I choose that. It's a coincidence; a series of events I'm not really engaged in. I don't know what I want to do with my life—I'm fourteen and my new friends won't stop asking what I've got "down there". I just want people to stop looking at me.

I enrol in floristry school. Our teacher talks about flowers that have male and female reproductive organs, and I hear the plants described in the same terms that the doctors used for me. Suddenly I'm six years old again, desperate for approval and afraid of being wrong in a way that we don't know how to fix. But, there's no whispering this time. Nobody looks concerned or disgusted.

Something clicks.

From Alstromeria to Zinnea, every flower has different physical traits and features and they are never hated for looking different. They are loved for it.
For the first time, I begin to think that maybe different doesn't mean wrong. Finding a new type of flower is cause for celebration, there's no need for hammering it into shape. There never was.

I am not a flower, but I can learn to treat myself like one. I can be exactly what I am and not have to apologise for the way I grow.

I am allowed to bloom.

Excerpts from *Microrretalos sobre Intersexualidad*

Rosalinda & Mary

Mary

I grew up believing I was abnormal because of my genital variations. I felt attracted to men, but I was very insecure because of the bullying I had endured throughout my childhood due to my somewhat masculine appearance and personality, until I had my first sexual relationship. After that, I had several partners who thought I was perfect and said they really liked my vulva just the way it was: different and special. I wouldn't trade my intersex vulva for a 'normal' vulva.

Crecí creyendo que era anormal debido a mis variaciones genitales. Me sentía atraída por hombres, pero sentía mucha inseguridad a causa del bullying que había sufrido durante toda la infancia por mi apariencia y personalidad un tanto masculinas,hasta que tuve mi primera relación sexual. Después de eso, tuve varias parejas a quienes yo les parecía perfecta y decían que les gustaba mucho mi vulva tal como era: diferente y especial. No cambiaría mi vulva intersex por una vulva "normal".

Rosalinda

When I was thirteen years old, my mother explained to my sister and me that she had to take us to the doctor because we were sick. However, my sister and I felt completely healthy and happy; we didn't understand why our mum was telling us we were sick. Then, the medical appointments started, and with them, our nightmare began. They subjected us to genital examinations where the doctors touched us and treated us like strange objects; they examined us naked in front of fifteen or more people, including doctors and practitioners. We both cried because of that and begged our mother not to take us to the doctor anymore.

One day, one of our sisters found out about our situation and began to humiliate me because I was growing a beard and body hair. The humiliation from her continued, without knowing what we were suffering at each medical appointment and ignoring the impact of her words. Not even people who were distant to me humiliated me as much as my own blood did.

Cuando tenía trece años, mi madre nos explicó a mí y a mi hermana que nos tenía que llevar al doctor porque estábamos enfermas. Sin embargo, mi hermana y yo nos sentíamos completamente sanas y felices, no entendíamos por qué mi mamá nos decía que estábamos enfermas. Entonces,empezaron las consultas médicas y, con ello, nuestra pesadilla. Nos hacían revisiones genitales en las que nos tocaban y nos trataban como cosas raras; nos desnudaban frente a quince o más personas, médicos y practicantes. Las dos llorábamos por todo eso y rogábamos a nuestra madre para que ya no nos llevará al doctor.

Un día, una de nuestras hermanas se enteró de nuestra situación y comenzó a humillarme porque me crecía barba y vello corporal. La humillación por parte de ella continuó, sin saber lo que sufríamos en cada cita médica e ignorando el efecto de sus palabras. Ni siquiera las personas poco cercanas a mí me humillaban tanto como lo hacía mi propia sangre.

Both pieces originally published in *Microrrelatos sobre Intersexualidad – México 2024 (Short Stories about Intersex)* by Xtagabe´ñe / Brújula Intersexual

Crecer - Growing up

A.A

Crecer muchas veces es difícil, dadas las situaciones que vivimos. El tiempo pasa y corre en nuestra contra. Crecemos y vemos, como si se tratara de una película, cómo otros niños juegan, hacen amigos, se caen, descubren lugares nuevos, nadan en el mar, pasean por el campo... Y tú, desde la ventana del hospital o de tu habitación, ves cómo creces y te haces adulto sintiendo que te han robado lo que muchos han tenido.

Crecer muchas veces da miedo y te escondes intentando que no ocurra.

¿Y a nosotros quién nos devuelve el tiempo?

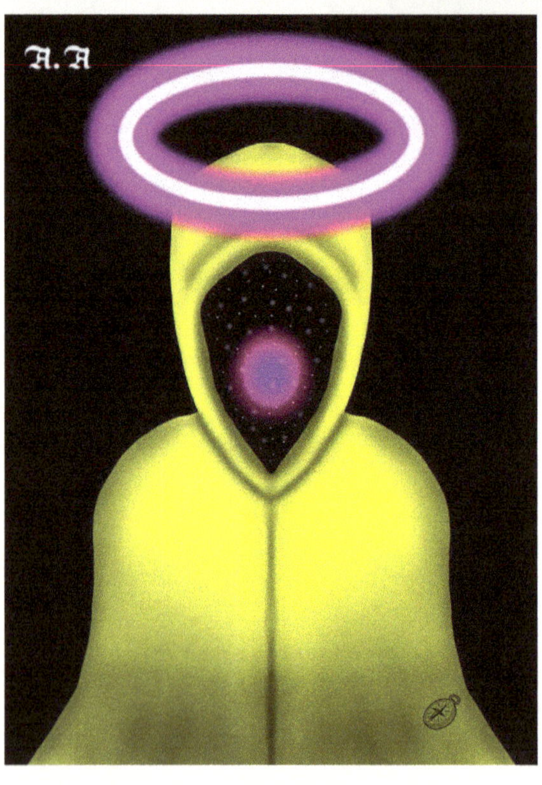

Growing up is often difficult given the situations we experience. Time passes and runs against us. We grow up and see, as if it were a movie, how other children play, make friends, fall down, discover new places, swim in the sea, walk in the countryside... and you, from the window of the hospital or your room, watch yourself grow and become an adult, feeling that you have been robbed of what many have had.

Growing up often scares you, and you hide, trying to avoid it.

And who will give us back the time?

Only a dead man should lose hope

Lee

Being an intersex person in remote areas is not an easy thing because only a few individuals understand, yet the greater part of the community never really understand anything to do with intersex people.

I grew up in the most remote areas of Zimbabwe, a place called Bhora where individuals don't own mobile phones and only the Village Headman has access to a phone. If people in the Village want to communicate with their relatives who are in urban areas, they have to go to the house of the Headman to make a call. When there is need to disseminate information, the Village boys beat a drum at a mountain and all the villagers gather at the mountain to hear the news. Even if there is a funeral or notification of an upcoming celebration, they use the same channel of communication.

I spent most of my childhood there and I was often regarded as taboo. Now that I am living in an urban setting, I am now using the advocacy strategies I have learnt by going back to that rural area where I grew up and making relationships with them as a way to educate and help them understand intersex issues. I also visit the Village Headman from time to time and now he has gotten to a point of actually explaining to others what being intersex means.

"Always remember that it's never too late to do things right."

My hope is that intersex people who grew up in a rural setting like mine should not neglect the places that they grew up in, but rather they should try by all means to give back information to the communities.

Always remember that it's never too late to do things right. Only a dead man should lose hope. As long as a person is alive then there is hope that all things will work out for good.

Soliloquio: Fragmentos de un Cuerpo Infinito

Julian

La escena está bañada en una suave luz de atardecer. La persona se encuentra de pie, apoyada en un bastón de madera. Se enfrenta a un espejo, que refleja tanto su cuerpo como su alma. Habla con un tono íntimo y melancólico, como si cada palabra fuera un fragmento.

Mirando al espejo con una expresión pensativa

Crecer... una palabra que para muchos significa avanzar, evolucionar. Pero para mí, es un entramado de contradicciones, un constante redescubrimiento de un ser que desafía las definiciones. Soy intersexual, una obra maestra de la naturaleza que no cabe en los marcos convencionales.

Se apoya más en el bastón, casi acariciándolo como un compañero fiel

Diez años. Diez largos años de consultas, exámenes y esperas interminables. Diez años de ser un rompecabezas que la medicina no podía resolver. Y al final, una respuesta. Un diagnóstico que vino como un susurro en la noche, cambiando la narrativa de mi existencia. Como un pintor añadiendo una sombra inesperada a un cuadro ya complejo.

Cierra los ojos por un momento, como si estuviera buscando las palabras adecuadas en lo profundo de su ser

Ser intersexual ya era un reto, una danza entre las sombras y la luz. Vivir en un cuerpo que confunde, que desafía las categorías y provoca miradas curiosas y juicios silenciosos. Y ahora, esta enfermedad. Cada paso que doy con este bastón es una prueba de mi fortaleza, un acto de resistencia en un mundo que no siempre entiende mi fragilidad.

Abre los ojos y se enfrenta al espejo con una mirada de acero

Pero en esta lucha, en esta dualidad, he encontrado una verdad más profunda. Crecer no es solo una cuestión de tiempo, es una transformación continua, un proceso de aceptación y de autoafirmación. Cada día, cada dolor, cada momento de duda es una pincelada en el lienzo de mi vida, una nota en la sinfonía de mi existencia.

Acaricia el bastón con una ternura inesperada

He aprendido a amar este cuerpo, este lienzo imperfecto que muchos no pueden comprender. He aprendido a aceptar una mente que a veces se siente atrapada entre dos mundos. Y, sobre todo, he aprendido que ser intersexual y vivir con una discapacidad no me define; me moldea, me embellece, me hace único.

Mirando al horizonte, con una intensidad que desafía la comprensión y la compasión

Soy más que las etiquetas que otros tratan de imponerme. Soy más que un diagnóstico, más que una condición. Soy una persona que ha crecido en la adversidad, que ha encontrado poesía en el dolor y belleza en la lucha. Y mientras continúo este viaje, sé que no estoy solo. Hay otros como yo, otros que también están creciendo, descubriendo su propia voz en el silencio, su propio poder en la vulnerabilidad.

Y con una sonrisa que refleja la paz interior y la esperanza, concluye

Así que sí, estoy creciendo. Cada día, cada momento, cada paso que doy con este bastón. Y esa, esa es mi verdadera obra de arte.

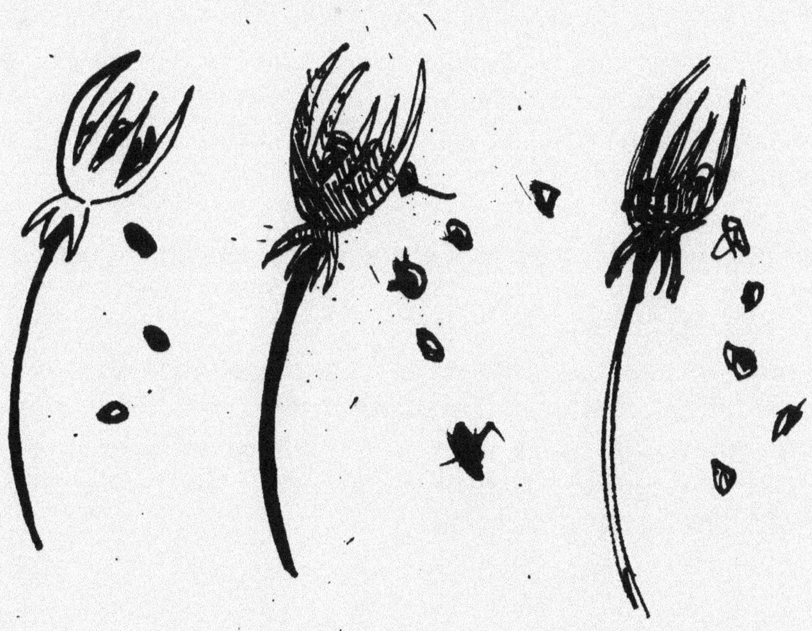

Soliloquy: Fragments of an Infinite Body

Julian

The scene is bathed in the soft light of sunset. The person stands, leaning on a wooden cane. They face a mirror, which reflects both their body and soul. They speak with an intimate, melancholic tone, as if each word is a fragment.

Looking into the mirror with a thoughtful expression

Growing... a word that, for many, means moving forward, evolving. But for me, it's a web of contradictions, a constant rediscovery of a being that defies definitions. I am intersex, a masterpiece of nature that doesn't fit into conventional frames.

Leans more on the cane, almost caressing it like a loyal companion

Ten years. Ten long years of consultations, exams, and endless waiting. Ten years of being a puzzle that medicine couldn't solve. And in the end, an answer. A diagnosis that came like a whisper in the night, changing the narrative of my existence. Like a painter adding an unexpected shadow to an already complex painting.

Closes their eyes for a moment, as if searching for the right words deep within themselves

Being intersex was already a challenge, a dance between shadows and light. Living in a body that confuses, that defies categories and provokes curious glances and silent judgements. And now, this illness. Every step I take with this cane is a testament to my strength, an act of resistance in a world that doesn't always understand my fragility.

Opens their eyes and faces the mirror with a steely gaze

But in this struggle, in this duality, I've found a deeper truth. Growing is not just a matter of time; it's a continuous transformation, a process of acceptance and self-affirmation. Each day, each pain, each moment of doubt is a brushstroke on the canvas of my life, a note in the symphony of my existence.

Gently caresses the cane with unexpected tenderness

I've learned to love this body, this imperfect canvas that many can't understand. I've learned to accept a mind that sometimes feels trapped between two worlds. And above all, I've learned that being intersex and living with a disability doesn't define me; it shapes me, beautifies me, makes me unique.

Looking toward the horizon, with an intensity that defies understanding and compassion

I am more than the labels others try to impose on me. I am more than a diagnosis, more than a condition. I am a person who has grown in adversity, who has found poetry in pain and beauty in the struggle. And as I continue this journey, I know I am not alone. There are others like me, others who are also growing, discovering their own voice in the silence, their own power in vulnerability.

And with a smile that reflects inner peace and hope, concludes

So yes, I am growing. Every day, every moment, every step I take with this cane. And that, that is my true work of art.

About the contributors

Some contributors have chosen to remain anonymous. We respect their wishes and have not published biographies of all contributors.

A.A

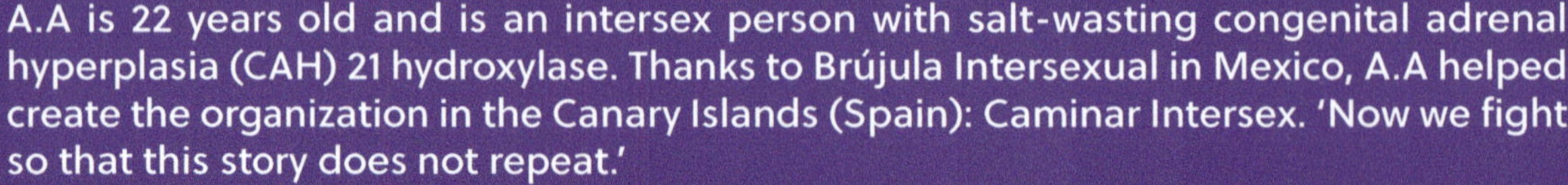

A.A is 22 years old and is an intersex person with salt-wasting congenital adrenal hyperplasia (CAH) 21 hydroxylase. Thanks to Brújula Intersexual in Mexico, A.A helped create the organization in the Canary Islands (Spain): Caminar Intersex. 'Now we fight so that this story does not repeat.'

Ayito

Ayito is from Argentina and is an artist and professor of Literature. Ayito is a trans person with a disability. Ayito is also the Director of Espacio Tolomocho, an organization dedicated to the art of LGBTI people with disabilities, and is a member of Argentina Intersex. Ayito enjoys dancing, drawing and painting. Instagram - @artedisca and @ espaciotolomocholgbti

Azucena

Azucena is from the municipality of El Fuerte, in the state of Sinaloa, Mexico and currently lives in the municipality of Sinaloa. Her intersex variation is congenital adrenal hyperplasia (CAH). She has a degree in Social Work and in Law. Azucena has been a collaborator of Brújula Intersexual since 2015 and her hobbies are listening to music, reading, exercising and taking care of her pets (two dogs).

Ciara

Ciara is 19 years old and is intersex. Ciara likes to draw in her free time and spend time with her family. She still hasn't decided what she would like to study; it's complicated because there are many university careers and she hasn't chosen one yet. However, she hopes to do her best in the career she chooses and continue growing.

Free

Free, originally from Oaxaca, Mexico, has a degree in Language Teaching (Spanish, English, French, and Zapotec). She met Brújula Intersexual in 2014, and one year later she became a collaborator of the same organisation. She has participated in various talks and events about intersex in Mexico, and her testimony entitled "An Orchid in a Rose Garden" was published on the website of Brújula Intersexual.

IR-Is 

IR-Is, born on April 12, 1994, in Caracas, Venezuela, is an intersex woman and environmental manager. As head of research at Intersex Venezuela since 2021, she advocates for intersex rights and environmental protection. She employs ethnobotany in her therapeutic approach and leads the Pira Verde Project.

ITSH 

Julian

Julian is an intersex person and university professor of Research Methodology originally from Caracas, Venezuela. A pioneer in Venezuelan intersex activism, he founded Intersex Venezuela, the first intersex organization in the country, in 2018. He participated in the first and second regional and Latin American conference of intersex people, contributing to the 2018 San Jose Declaration.

Juniper Fox 

Juniper Fox is a Pacific Northwest born, Eastern Washington transplant. Juniper is 24 and is the founder of a high school's LGBTQIA+ Alliance, which opened the door to their Activism and Advocacy surrounding Intersex Rights, & other marginalised LGBTQIA+ communities. Outside of that, Juniper is a Freelance Visual Artist.

Kali 

Kali Castro is a medium, illustrator, and teacher. They hold a Bachelor's degree in Education and are currently pursuing a Master's degree in Human Rights at the University of Lanús. They are a member of Orgullo Disca, Bordando Disidencias, and Orgullo Loco. Kali resides in Lomas de Zamora, Buenos Aires. https://www.instagram.com/_fuegue/

Kon Zer 

Kon Zer is a 26-year-old intersex woman from Greece and part of Intersex Greece. She has studied Chemistry but also has great interest in art. She is always trying to find creative ways to express herself and tell her story.

Lee 

Lee is an intersex person born in the year 1996. Lee is Zimbabwean and lives in the remote areas of Zimbabwe. His greatest passion is to write articles as well as poems and he wishes to continue his education.

M. Hill 

M. Hill is an intersex teenager from the United States. Passionate about writing, he always makes time to pursue creative interests and pours his heart and soul into these endeavors. He hopes you enjoy his poem.

Marel 

Marel is 39 years old from Mexico and was diagnosed at birth with Turner Syndrome. Marel has connected with people who have the same condition as her. However, 3 years ago, she became aware of her intersexuality and discovered the Brújula Intersexual web page. That encouraged her to share her story with Turner Syndrome and intersexuality. She completed two bachelor's degrees and a master's degree. Currently, she has a stable job and is self-sufficient.

Mary 

Mary is an intersex woman from Guadalajara, Jalisco, Mexico and is a collaborator at Brújula Intersexual. She loves nature and science.

Max Aurora 

Max is 30 years old living in Wurundjeri country in Australia. They are an intersex person with XX male syndrome, and identify as non binary / trans femme. They are studying Music Therapy in Melbourne and lead a band called 'Max Aurora & The Southern Lights'. Instagram - @maxauroramusic; https://linktr.ee/maxauroramusic

Mel Kurutta 

Mel Kurutta is an artist and activist for the human rights of intersex people. Their art, chameleonic and impulsive, mirrors their experience as an intersex person, lesbian and disabled. Since 2020, they are part of the InterseXioni collective, as a member of the Intersex Youth Group and the Executive. Personal link tree - https://linktr.ee/melkurutta

Mouse  

Mouse is from Australia and New Zealand, and currently living in Austria. He is studying floristry and works as a lived experience peer educator for youth mental health, and is the designated cat sitter for the neighbourhood's felines.

Nico 

Nico is a 7-year-old intersex kid from Mexico.

Noor Alom 

Noor Alom is a young Bangladeshi intersex rights activist and co-founder of Intersex Bangladesh, an intersex-led youth organization. Despite facing numerous unnecessary and unconsented surgeries that deprived him of basic human rights like education, healthcare, and employment, Noor is dedicated to promoting intersex rights in Bangladesh and Asia.

Otto Etraud 

Otto Etraud/Toto Duarte (Chile, 1992) is an illustrator, graphic artist, and muralist. They studied Graphic Design at the University of Valparaíso. Their work explores narratives on sexual diversity, gender, political identities, emotions, and everyday life. Since 2020, they have been painting murals in public spaces and secret locations, working with various communities, art producers, and brands. They are currently working on the script for an audiovisual project about intersexuality and collaborating on related projects. Otto's work can be found at www.ottoetraud.com.

Ranzie Orcena 

Ranzie Magalona Orcena is 26 years old, a member of Intersex Philippines and is a licensed pharmacist. "Being intersex isn't just a part of me, it's all of me. For Intersex Filipinos, let us have the courage to embrace our uniqueness."

Rosalinda 

Rosalinda is an intersex woman from Guadalajara, Jalisco, Mexico and is a collaborator at Brújula Intersexual.

Tobias Kenny 

Tobias (he/him/ia) is a takatāpui person from Aotearoa New Zealand. He has whakapapa from the Māori iwi of Kai Tahu and Te Ātiawa. He works in rainbow/queer spaces and is also studying Anthropology and Te Reo Māori (Māori language). He also likes designing and playing tabletop role-playing games, crocheting and reading.

Vanessy 

Vanessy is a 10-year-old intersex girl who is in the 4th grade of primary school. Her male classmates argue over wanting Vanessy on their team because she is passionate about playing soccer, and they call her the "Star Player." Her favorite hobby is building structures with LEGO. She really likes tropical fruits and her favorite fast food is pizza. She wants to study engineering at university.

Yela 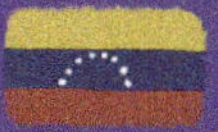

www.ingramcontent.com/pod-product-compliance
Lightning Source LLC
Chambersburg PA
CBHW041210100726
47911CB00017B/912

* 9 7 8 0 6 4 5 6 7 2 6 2 6 *